# Can You Count in the Dark?

You bet you can!

by Annie Ingle

illustrated by
Denise Brunkus

## How to use this book:

First count things with the light on.
Then when you see the * symbol, switch off the light.
Switch it back on after you've counted in the dark.
Proceed in this fashion all the way through the book.

**RANDOM HOUSE 🏠 NEW YORK**

Text copyright © 1993 by Random House, Inc. Illustrations copyright © 1993 by Denise Brunkus. All rights reserved under International and Pan-American Copyright Conventions. Published in the United States by Random House, Inc., New York, and simultaneously in Canada by Random House of Canada Limited, Toronto.
*Library of Congress Cataloging-in-Publication Data*: Brunkus, Denise. Can you count in the dark?  p. cm.  SUMMARY: As a boy roams around his house and yard, illustrations and rhyming text present various items from one moon to ten stars. Parts of the pictures are only visible when the lights are out.  ISBN 0-679-84195-4
1. Counting—Juvenile literature.  2. Glow-in-the-dark books—Specimens.  [1. Counting.  2. Glow-in-the-dark books.  3. Toy and movable books.]
I. Title.  QA113.B78  1993  513.2'11—dc20  [E]  92-30145  Manufactured in Taiwan  10 9 8 7 6 5 4 3 2 1

1 doorbell,
1 mailbox,
1 birdhouse, up high,
1 moon shining brightly up in the sky. ✳

2 baseballs,
2 bats,
2 family cars,
2 glowing sneakers covered with stars.✱

3 saucers,
3 cups,
3 books on the chair,
3 magnets shining on the Frigidaire.*

4 baskets,
4 pots,
4 pictures on the walls,
4 things to juggle,
Yes! 4 glowing balls. *

5 shining street lamps shed 5 pools of light. ✳

6 cushions,
6 apples, half of them red,

6 glowing fish who want to be fed. *

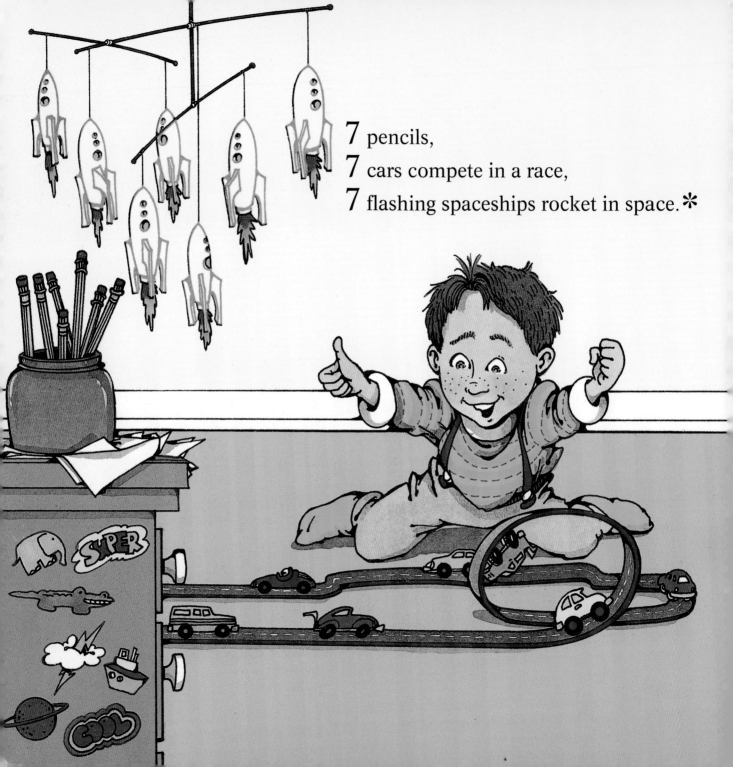

7 pencils,
7 cars compete in a race,
7 flashing spaceships rocket in space. *

8 jacks,
8 comics I've already read,
8 gleaming cats' eyes under my bed.*

9 tulips, 9 crocuses, closed up tight,

**9** busy fireflies swarm in the night.✳

**10** windowpanes,
**10** biscuits set down in a dish,

**10** stars in the sky — let's make a wish!✱

I wish I could count everything in this book
all over again . . . *in the dark!* *

| | |
|---|---|
| 1 | moon |
| 2 | sneakers |
| 3 | magnets |
| 4 | balls |
| 5 | street lamps |
| 6 | fish |
| 7 | spaceships |
| 8 | cats' eyes |
| 9 | fireflies |
| 10 | stars |